Twenty Keys For Me

Twenty Keys For Me

The Relentless Pursuit for Success

Joel Freedman

Published by Tablo

Copyright © Joel Freedman 2020.
Published in 2020 by Tablo Publishing.

All rights reserved.

This book or any portion thereof may not be reproduced or used in any manner whatsoever without the express written permission of the author except for the use of brief quotations in a book review.

Publisher and wholesale enquiries: orders@tablo.io

20 21 22 23 LSC 10 9 8 7 6 5 4 3 2 1

Table of Contents

FOREWORD	1
EMBRACE FAILURE	3
THRIVE ON THE ANSWER "NO"	5
FOLLOW UP WITH PURPOSE	7
RESPOND TO OUTREACH	9
"BIG PICTURE VIEW, SMALL PICTURE FOCUS"	11
ENSURE PRODUCTIVITY	13
CONTROL YOUR POINT OF VIEW	15
COMMUNICATE FOR TODAY	17
AVOID MULTITASKING	19
UNDER 10 MINUTE RULE	21
CREATE MORE VALUABLE TIME	23
KEEP A FRESH MIND	25
FIND A REASON TO SUCCEED	27
DO WHAT YOU ARE PASSIONATE ABOUT	29
ROOT FOR SUCCESS	31
KEEP A CLEAN DIGITAL TATTOO	33
BE KIND	35
PRACTICE EMAIL RESTRAINT	37
BE POSITIVE	39
CRAVE ACCOMPLISHMENT	41

FOREWORD

Twenty Keys For Me is a book I wrote for myself during the COVID-19 pandemic. A couple weeks into the stay at home order, I began to realize everything I had worked for over the last few years was going to crumble before my eyes. Managing two businesses in arguably the most severely impacted industries (Leisure Travel - Cruise Line & Casino), and developing a third business manufacturing a new appliance for the Coffee Service Industry, I saw myself being out of work for quite some time.

I had this fear that I would become rusty in my operational skill sets built over my 15 year career - a fear that I would develop bad habits that could result in a lack of drive and possibly negativity. I needed to do something that I could control because the rest of my professional life was dependent on other's decisions that would allow me to work.

Twenty Keys For Me is a reminder of how I got to where I was pre-pandemic. I figured if I could just keep these skills fresh, starting all over again might be a little easier.

This book is not written to provide a story or to consume your time. It's actually the opposite. I tried to avoid as much story telling as possible and get straight to the point. In my opinion, your time is valuable and any book offering professional advice should take that into consideration.

My hope for you in reading this book is that at least one of these keys offers you something new to put into practice and if not, may the keys simply serve as a reminder of skill sets you already possess. Enjoy.

Recommendation for Reading Style:

- Read one key per day (only on workdays)
- Read in the morning before you start your workday
- Read with an open mind and reflect on personal experiences

EMBRACE FAILURE

Context

Why are people afraid to fail? It is a tough question to answer because everyone is different. Could it be because when we were younger, failure had consequences? Could it be because we care too much about what others think, and failure is embarrassing? Could it be because failing is disappointing?

This fear of failure can prevent you from attempting to accomplish great things.

Guidance

Failure is a learning tool to move forward. Many of the great products/services we enjoy today were developed through "trial and error" - a practice that uses failure as a means to find success. Think about failure differently. Embrace failure; it is part of life. You are going to fail at things both in your personal and your professional life. It simply comes with the territory of being an active member in society.

Don't allow the idea that you may fail to get in the way of pursuing something you believe in. Don't allow the thoughts of others to stop you from trying. Use the negative energy from those who judge you as fuel to prove them wrong.

Turn the fear of failure into the fear of not trying.

THRIVE ON THE ANSWER "NO"

Context

Today in sales, or any role that requires you to be dependent on other's decision making, one of the most difficult hurdles to cross is simply getting a response. People are just too busy, and our communication style allows for easy avoidance. The task of pushing for an answer becomes even more difficult if you're afraid of the answer being "No." Hearing or reading the answer "No" repeatedly can wear on your confidence, thus impacting your courage to even reach out.

Guidance

If you are someone who cannot bear to hear the answer "no," try to view the response as a success. Getting an answer is a win, even if the response is "no." Sure, a rejection is not what you wanted to receive; but think about how difficult it was, or could have been, to get that answer. An uninterested prospect just saved you a great deal of time in following up, and wondering if they will be a buyer in whatever you're selling.

Thrive on the answer "no" as energy for the next contact - view this "no" as THEIR loss for not buying, and get excited to offer it to their competitor. Do not let "no," discourage you from your goal.

The answer "No" is better than no answer at all.

FOLLOW UP WITH PURPOSE

Context

"Following up" is an important skill set. So important, in fact, that companies continue to invest big money into tools that help their employees manage outreach efforts.

No matter what your role is, you will encounter messages that go unanswered. It is a difficult task to get a response - something that is important to you, may not be important to others. Another hurdle is that the number of competing messages an individual receives per day is growing. This will result in a strong likelihood that you will need to follow up.

Guidance

First off, you need to remember to follow up on unanswered outreach. Set reminders in your calendar, review your sent messages from the week prior, or use one of the CRM (Customer Relationship Management) tools that may be available to you.

Secondly, be sure to follow up with purpose. Try to not follow up with the typical "just checking back in" message. Put some purpose into the follow up by adding some additional value. This added value can be a monetary benefit, it can express a missed opportunity, or you can further play into what you know the recipient's interests are.

Encourage a response by following up with purpose.

RESPOND TO OUTREACH

Context

Today, you are inundated with different ways for sales professionals to get in touch. Phone Calls, Text Messages, Emails, Social Media Messages, Mailers, etc... a majority of which require time to read. Thus, it is easy for you to ignore. Overtime you can become conditioned to disregard the outreach. This behavior can lead to missed opportunities, delays in productivity, and even carry over to ignoring messages from other individuals in your professional or personal life.

Guidance

Answer as many phone calls, emails, texts, or social media outreaches as possible. If you are not interested in what is being sold to you, just politely say "No." Allow the person on the other end of the outreach to move on with their efforts. Advise them to remove you from their marketing list if you think you will never be interested in what they are selling. This will be one less marketing outreach to answer.

If the communication is too long-winded and you do not have time to read through it, let the person know. Maybe they will summarize it for you.

It is likely you do not want to be pitched, but try to always keep an open mind. While you may not be in the market for what is being sold to you today, down the road you could have a need for it. Understanding what is being sold will help you remember it for possible future use.

Responding is polite and productive. Help push productivity.

"BIG PICTURE VIEW, SMALL PICTURE FOCUS"

Context

When starting a new business or a new project, a pattern typically occurs. First, you think about the end product. Then you begin the planning phase, considering all of the possible steps required to reach your determined goal. Some people drop off from pursuing this goal when these steps are too intimidating to even take on. Others jump into the project and abort mission upon hitting the first or second challenge in development.

Guidance

Approaching this new initiative with a "Big Picture View, Small Picture Focus" could help you see your way to the end product. Having a Big Picture View means to dream about the product or service potential. Dreaming will help fuel the motivation to continue as you come against challenges within the development process.

Having a Small Picture Focus is about not looking at all the challenges ahead and focusing on just the next two steps in the development process. Put 80 percent of your focus on the development task at hand and the other 20 percent of focus on the step to follow. This will allow for smooth transitions in the development process and can help limit challenges as you progress.

Dream Big, Focus Small.

ENSURE PRODUCTIVITY

Context

In your day to day work life, you may become bogged down with maintenance work. This is routine work that is required to keep your business operating as it should to make money. For example, you secure a great new customer. This customer begins buying your product, but will begin to require attention in the way of customer service, paperwork, problem solving, etc... This maintenance work becomes time consuming and can prevent you from being productive in growing the business.

Guidance

Adopt a rule to make at least one outreach per day to a new customer or existing customer for the purposes of increasing revenue. Everyone's earnings are different, but think about a daily earning figure that is important to you. Let's say you want to make an extra $300 per workday. Do not stop your day until you make that $300 earning potential outreach.

Make sure your days are productive. Servicing business you already have is important for business retention, but you need to strive for growth.

Always be moving forward.

CONTROL YOUR POINT OF VIEW

Context

Often when building a new business, it takes time to see any true financial benefit. For this reason, many people need to work additional full-time jobs or continue managing other businesses that are making money. After all, you have bills to pay. This can create a view point that the new business you are working to develop is a "side project." The side project point of view can be the demise of the business. It is easy to ignore side projects and it is hard to justify investing money to get the new venture going or sustaining.

Guidance

If you want to see this new business become successful and generate a viable source of income, you cannot view it as a "Side Project." Shift your mindset and view this new business as being your key to financial freedom. If your point of view is in the right place, you will make the time available to do whatever is necessary to get the business in a position for success.

Your viewpoint will control your behavior. Your behavior will control your results.

COMMUNICATE FOR TODAY

Context

Recent studies have shown that the average human's attention span is now only 8 seconds. This is down from the 12 seconds determined in the year 2000. Our communication style has also changed over the last twenty plus years, shifting more to communicating via emails and text messages rather than phone conversations. This combination is playing a large role in our inability to get responses.

Guidance

Unfortunately, the solution here isn't as easy as just picking up the phone and calling. The problem is that your audience not only prefers to send digital communication themselves, but they also prefer to receive communication digitally. Thus, you need to work within this communication style framework, but tweak your message structure. Make your messages easy to read, visually appealing, and concise.

- Stay clear of long paragraphs
- Get to the point
- Use bullets whenever possible
- Use bold font to call out an important message
- Always reread your message to make sure you are getting the point across and eliminate any wasteful wording

Less is more. Be concise and efficient.

AVOID MULTITASKING

Context

The art of multitasking is something that is mastered by very few. In your job or in managing your own business, it is likely that you will be asked to balance multiple tasks at the same time. Without dedicated focus, the work may not be completed properly or at the highest level of quality.

Guidance

Simply put, try to avoid multitasking as much as possible. Focus on one thing at a time. If you're writing an email to a co-worker, focus on that email and block out other tasks or distractions until the email is completed. If you are having a conversation with a client, co-worker, or anybody for that matter, give this person your undivided attention. You will find that you will complete tasks faster and the quality will improve if your attention is not being spread across multiple tasks at one time.

The art of multitasking is to actually focus on one task at a time in order to allow you to complete multiple tasks throughout the day.

You do not have to multitask to complete multiple tasks.

UNDER 10 MINUTE RULE

Context

Throughout your day, small unplanned tasks are going to enter your workload. Whether it's an email requesting you to send a document, entering a sale into the system, etc... These tasks are easy to delay due to their simple nature, and your desire to work on the larger, more important tasks at hand. By putting off these tasks, they will compound on top of one another and could become stressful.

Guidance

By practicing the "Art of Multitasking," you are ensuring that you are not introducing any small unplanned tasks, until you are ready to receive them. Once you move on, and you begin to check your messages, do so by applying the "Under 10 Minute Rule." This rule suggests that if the newly introduced task can be completed in under 10 minutes, complete the task immediately. By employing this strategy, you will prevent the work from piling up to a point that could cause an increased level of stress, therefore increasing your overall productivity.

Don't let the small tasks weigh on you like large tasks.

CREATE MORE VALUABLE TIME

Context

If time is something money cannot buy, then how do you put a value on it? The value is different for everyone. Throughout the course of your day, the activities of others and yourself can have an impact on your time. As the day moves on, the delays can be mounting unless you step in and manage the day properly to make up for any lost time.

Guidance

Appreciate time and show it the respect it deserves. At the start of each week, you should look at your calendar and plan the days accordingly. Simply being aware of your schedule can help you manage your time and activity better. Here are a few things you can do to help create more valuable time:

- Block out time on your schedule each day that will provide an opportunity for you to work efficiently with limited distractions.
- Steer clear of multitasking.
- Make as many of your phone calls as possible during your commute to and from work.
- Evaluate your reoccurring meetings:
  - Are they productive?
  - Can they be shortened?
  - Can anybody be excused from them?
  - Do they start and end on time?

Time management is a tremendous skill set. It will help you get the most out of your day and make up for the time taken by others.

You may not be able to buy more time, but you can create more valuable time.

KEEP A FRESH MIND

Context

Have you ever reached a point in your workday where it is hard to come up with the appropriate words in an email or conversation? Or you find yourself staring at your computer wondering what file you were just searching for? These are signs that your mind is tired. When your mind is tired, you may make errors in your work and will find certain tasks are taking you longer to complete than usual.

Guidance

Our minds are functioning at their best shortly after we wake up from a good night of sleep. Thus, it is best to prioritize your workday by beginning with the tasks that require an increased level of thinking. A good way to do this is to clear your schedule from any possible distractions that might interfere with completing the task. Push meetings, or work that is dependent on other's help, to the afternoon hours if you can. The socialization in the afternoon could help keep your energy levels up. As your day goes on, if you begin to show signs that your mind is becoming tired, do not try to push through it. Rather, you are better off mixing in something that gives your mind a break for 20-30 minutes. The 20-30-minute recharge will make up for itself with more productive work.

A fresh mind is a productive mind.

FIND A REASON TO SUCCEED

Context

Striving for success can be exhausting. Sometimes it is difficult to stay motivated. Many times, you need to see your way through difficult hurdles along the way. If you don't have something providing you motivation to succeed, it is easy to let yourself down and call it quits.

Guidance

It is important to constantly remind yourself of why you are striving for success. Whether it is to take care of your family, to improve upon a problem, etc., try to find that reason for success beyond your own personal well-being. Again, it is easy to let yourself down. It is hard to let down others, especially those you love. Finish this statement for yourself, "I want to be successful because…" Write the answer down somewhere and reflect on it anytime you feel a lack of motivation to succeed.

Working for a purpose can lead to greater success and personal fulfillment.

DO WHAT YOU ARE PASSIONATE ABOUT

Context

Upon graduating college, typically the goal is to find a job that suits your degree. The pressure to begin earning an income might cause you to accept the first offer you receive, rather than searching for a job that provides meaningful work. As the years go on, you may find yourself just working for a paycheck and not enjoying the work you do. This can have an impact on your overall quality of life.

Guidance

Think about your day. It is likely that work-related activities consume half, if not the majority of your time awake. Ask yourself if you truly enjoy what you do for a living. Are you passionate about your work? If the answer is no, you need to think about how you can get there. Begin by exploring what you dislike about your work. Is it the industry? Is it the work itself? Is it the people that you work with? Does your work interfere with your personal life and cause resentment? Whatever the reason may be, it is important to identify it and begin taking action. Enjoying your work can lead to tremendous personal and financial rewards over time.

Do what you are passionate about and turn every waking hour into something you enjoy doing.

ROOT FOR SUCCESS

Context

Jealously is a powerful emotion and one that can sometimes cause you to root for others to fail. After-all, misery loves company. Seeing others have what you want can be a difficult thing.

Guidance

Root for people to succeed and celebrate it with them. The change from jealousy to happiness could result in more success for yourself. If you cannot help yourself from being jealous, channel the jealous energy as motivation to find your own success. If you root for others to succeed, you will find yourself being surrounded by people who root for you to succeed as well. Most of us perform better when we have people rooting for us, rather than people rooting against us. Consider in sports, a "Home-field Advantage." Teams tend to preform better at home than they do on the road. There are a few reasons for this:

1. They are playing in a familiar atmosphere
2. They have a stadium full of fans cheering them on
3. They have motivation to perform at a higher level to reward the audience for their support

Create your own "Home-field Advantage." Root for success.

KEEP A CLEAN DIGITAL TATTOO

Context

Social Media - a means for people to share facts, opinions, beliefs and lies with the world. Your activity on social media can be viewed as a digital tattoo. Employers, customers, competitors, business partners, etc.. can view your social media activity and make decisions based on how you represent yourself.

Guidance

When using Social Media, it is important to use the platform as it is intended to be used and always be considerate of what you're sharing on that platform. The world is your audience and you depend on the world to help you find success in your journey. Some fundamental things to steer clear from posting on social media:

- Inappropriate pictures
- Rumors/Lies/Hate
- Disgruntled complaints
- Profanity
- Controversial topics that can polarizing (such as politics).

Your social media should be as professional as your resume. If you would not say it in an interview, do not post it on social media.

Your digital tattoo is one that you will need to wear for life. Make sure you are proud of it today, tomorrow, and five years from now.

BE KIND

Context

As you move through your career, you are likely to encounter some people that are just not kind. These individuals are typically frustrated personally, professionally, or both, and have grown to be unpleasant over time. This foul attitude is probably what is now preventing them from escaping whatever it is that is causing the frustration.

Guidance

Be kind. Being kind to others no matter their title, is a simple task that requires zero talent and one that will be rewarded over time. Nobody likes a mean-spirited individual and these people end up getting managed out of good organizations. This does not make you a pushover. Being kind will help you connect better with others, which, in turn, could lead to promotions, additional sales, etc...

Follow the old saying: treat others the way you wish to be treated.

PRACTICE EMAIL RESTRAINT

Context

Have you ever been frustrated with a situation at work and want to send everyone involved an email that will set them straight? If you have been working long enough, you have likely had this experience. You probably have sent that nasty email a few times. It is hard to resist, especially when you are on the receiving end of one, and you want to fight back.

Guidance

Type the email in all your fury. Enjoy it and get it out of your system. Writing the email can be therapeutic. Do not immediately send the email. Once the email is completed, save it to drafts and reread it the next day. If you still feel the same way after you reviewed it in a calmer state of mind, begin to ask yourself some questions:

- Does the email accomplish something positive?
- Does it steer clear of being offensive?
- Will you get a positive response?
- Can the email be viewed by anybody not on the distribution list?

If the answer to all of these questions is "Yes", then send away; but if the answer is "No" for any of these questions, you should revise the email or not send it at all.

Try to avoid words that intensify adjectives ('Very" or "Really"). This will help soften the message.

Nasty emails can lead to nasty results.

BE POSITIVE

Context

Whether you run your own business or work for a company, you will experience frustrating results or situations. This frustration can build up inside of you overtime and cause a pessimistic attitude. A negative state of mind could destroy your business, or become an issue for the company you work for. In any company, a negative attitude can be contagious and infect the rest of the organization over time. These people end up getting referred to as a "Cancer within the Organization." The company then needs to work to get all the cancer out of its system.

Guidance

Always try to maintain a optimistic attitude. You can do this by trying to find positives in all outcomes. Don't let the frustrating results take away your pride. Surround yourself with other positive individuals. When you encounter somebody with a negative attitude, challenge them to think differently rather than let them get away with the negative outlook. A positive state of mind will lead to greater endurance in whatever you are doing and will allow you to better tackle challenges as they arise.

A positive mind is a healthy mind.

CRAVE ACCOMPLISHMENT

Context

Have you ever had the feeling that you are just not moving forward? You feel a lack of progress, control, and you may even be going backwards in achieving your goal. Perhaps you hit a roadblock and the current market conditions are making it tough to get past. Or maybe the people you are depending on to help accomplish your goal are the roadblock. This is life - variable market conditions, and depending on others to make decisions favorable to your well-being, are things you will never entirely get away from.

Guidance

If you find your confidence taking a hit from this staleness in your professional life, you need to do something to combat it. Think about things you can accomplish in your personal life that you would be proud of and do not depend on others to succeed. For example, look towards fitness. Losing weight or achieving specific fitness goals are solely dependent on you. If you want to lose 20 pounds, set a realistic timeline and a plan of attack to get it done. How can you depend on others if you cannot depend on yourself? Accomplishing personal goals can help boost your self-confidence and carry over into your professional life. The key is, you must crave the accomplishment and achieve the goal no matter what.

Believe in yourself and increase your confidence by accomplishing something only you can control.

It is never too late to unlock your potential.

Lightning Source UK Ltd.
Milton Keynes UK
UKHW040936201020
371904UK00001B/250